CONTENTS

INTRODUCTION   5

NURSING SERVICES   15

MUNITIONETTES AND WOMEN WAR WORKERS   31

ON THE LAND   43

IN UNIFORM   51

DEMOB AND LEGACIES   59

FURTHER READING   63

INDEX   64

WOMEN OF BRITAIN SAY — "GO!"

Published by the PARLIAMENTARY RECRUITING COMMITTEE, London. Poster No. 75   Printed by HILL, SIFFKEN & Co. (L.P.A. Ltd.), Grafton Works, London, N. W. (374) 25 M. 3/15

W THE
FIRST WORLD WAR

Neil Storey & Molly Housego

SHIRE PUBLICATIONS

Published in Great Britain in 2014 by Shire Publications Ltd,
PO Box 883, Oxford OX1 9PL, United Kingdom.
PO Box 3985, New York, NY 10185-3983, USA.
E-mail: shire@shirebooks.co.uk   www.shirebooks.co.uk

A CIP catalogue record for this book is available from the
British Library.

Shire Library no. 575   •   ISBN-13: 978 0 74780 752 0

Neil Storey and Molly Housego have asserted their right
under the Copyright, Designs and Patents Act, 1988, to
be identified as the authors of this book.

Designed by Tony Truscott Designs, Sussex, UK
Typeset in Perpetua and Gill Sans.
Printed in China through World Print Ltd.

14 15 16 17 18   13 12 11 10 9 8 7 6 5 4

COVER IMAGE
Cover design by Peter Ashley: image from *Our Hospital ABC*
by Joyce Dennys, publisher John Lane, The Bodley Head,
1916. Back cover detail: Women's Land Army Proficiency
badge (Ron Franklyn).

TITLE PAGE IMAGE
'Pat', a Voluntary Aid Detachment Nurse, 1914.

CONTENTS PAGE IMAGE
Two young members of the Women's Army Auxiliary
Corps, 1917.

ACKNOWLEDGEMENTS
We are grateful for the help and support of many people in
the production of this book. In particular we would like to
record our thanks to: Geoff Caulton; Dr Stephen Cherry;
Rod Flood; Ron and Jenny Franklyn; Robert Skinner;
the late Olive Learner; Margaret Newman at the Royal
Navy Museum, Portsmouth; the Norfolk Federation of
Women's Institutes; Helen Pugh at the British Red Cross
Museum, London; Ted Round; Diane Storey; Helen Tovey
and all the team at *Family Tree* Magazine; Pamela Willis and
Esmee Salkend at the Museum of the Order of St John,
London; and the staff of the Imperial War Museum
Department of Photographs. The archive reference
numbers for Imperial War Museum (IWM) images are
noted at the end of the relevant captions.

IMPERIAL WAR MUSEUM COLLECTIONS
Some of the photos in this book come from the Imperial
War Museum's huge collections, which cover all aspects
of conflict involving Britain and the Commonwealth since
the start of the twentieth century. These rich resources
are available online to search, browse and buy at
www.iwmcollections.org.uk. In addition to Collections
Online, you can visit the Visitor Rooms, where you can
explore over 8 million photographs, thousands of hours of
moving images, the largest sound archive of its kind in the
world, thousands of diaries and letters written by people
in wartime, and a huge reference library. To make an
appointment, call (020) 7416 5320,
or e-mail mail@iwm.org.uk
Imperial War Museum www.iwm.org.uk

Shire Publications is supporting the Woodland Trust, the UK's leading woodland conservation charity, by funding the dedication of trees.

INTRODUCTION

WHEN WAR was declared in 1914 it was greeted with cheering in the streets and general celebration. Thousands of men were mobilised from the Army and Navy Reserves and the Territorial Force, and thousands more enlisted. Britain was swept with flag-waving jingoism befitting its great Empire, and those who had been raised in the patriotic ethos – be they men or women – wanted, indeed considered it their duty, to do *something* for the war effort.

The first mass effort on the home front saw special high profile Red Cross fund-raising events staged and 'the Romance of the Red Cross' became common parlance in both press and periodicals. Soon more women than ever before were getting involved with other funds, both in street collections and getting hands on helping the likes of Belgian Refugees and at the YMCA 'huts' set up to provide canteens and comforts for the military both home and abroad. All of these activities were considered perfectly acceptable to those raised in Victorian and Edwardian society. The iconography of womanhood was also a common feature in early war posters whereby British men were called to enlist to defend and protect British women from violation by the hoards of invading Huns; a concept made more real and dreaded after press coverage spoke of 'the Rape of Belgium', accompanied by accounts of suitably lurid atrocities committed against the women as the enemy forces took the country. By far the most iconic of all the images of this period and theme was the simplest: the beautiful mother, children around her, gazing from the window as the soldiers march by. The image was reassuring and proud; she could cope and carry on and thus the simple legend of the poster was 'Women of Britain say – "Go!"'

Other posters asked women to consider, 'Why is your best boy not in khaki?' The onus was then placed on the woman to challenge her sweetheart or husband why he was not doing his bit. At this time women began gathering on streets and presenting men who were not in uniform with white feathers as a mark of cowardice. After a number of incidents in which men who were in fact 'doing their bit' but were still in civilian clothes were attacked, lapel

Opposite:
The famous
'Women of Britain
say – "Go!"'
poster of 1914.
(IWM PST 2763)

5

Collecting for the
Belgian Refugee
Distress Fund
at the entrance
to Newmarket
racecourse
in 1914.
(IWM Q 53361)

Why was your
best boy not
in khaki?
(IWM PST 4903)

TO THE
YOUNG WOMEN OF LONDON

Is your "Best Boy" wearing
Khaki? If not don't **YOU
THINK** he should be?

If he does not think that you
and your country are worth
fighting for—do you think he
is **WORTHY** of you?

Don't pity the girl who is
alone—her young man is
probably a soldier—fighting
for her and her country—
and for **YOU.**

If your young man neglects his duty to his
King and Country, the time may come when
he will **NEGLECT YOU.**

Think it over—then ask him to

JOIN THE ARMY TO-DAY

Printed by David Allen & Sons Ltd., Harrow, London, etc.

badges and identity cards were rapidly
produced for those involved in war work,
and armbands, rosettes and badges were
given to those who had newly volunteered
for the forces. Presentation of white
feathers continued throughout the war and
was reinvigorated with bitterness after
women started to lose their 'best boys' in
action. Even those who had served but had
been discharged through injury or sickness
and who were no longer in uniform or
showing any visible sign of their injury
were given white feathers; soon they too
were issued with the distinctive Silver War
Badge to denote their status and prevent
such occurrences.

In 1914 the National Union of
Women's Suffrage Societies, which had
been passionately campaigning for the right
of women to have the vote, suspended its
militant action to allow a concentration on
the war effort. However, the ensuing units
raised by suffragists or considered to have
suffragist interests were, for the most part,

treated with disdain by the military authorities. British society was engrained with Victorian and Edwardian values and although the suffrage associations were undoubtedly patriotic and were led by women with middle-, high-class and aristocratic backgrounds, for many these early women's units had pushed the moral standards too far. There were many haughty cries in gentlemen's clubs of 'Whatever next!' – then they would notice their niece or close family friend had joined. The situation was not helped by the lack of co-ordination in the women's war effort groups and soon a host of small groups established by women of similar backgrounds with similar aims were springing up across the country.

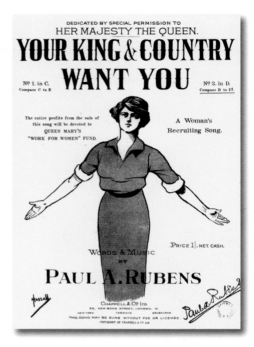

'Your King and Country Want You', a woman's recruiting song sheet of 1914.

The first in the field were Decima Moore and the militant and influential suffragette the Hon Evelina Haverfield, who raised the Women's Emergency Corps to provide feeding centres for soldiers and refugees. Then came the Women's Volunteer Reserve, sponsored by the Marchioness of Londonderry, Marchioness of Titchfield and the Countess of Pembroke and Montgomery; there was even Mrs Dawson Scott's Women's Defence Relief Corps. Some units had been long established, such as the First Aid Nursing Yeomanry (FANY), raised in 1907, and the Women's Sick and Wounded Convoy Corps, raised by the redoubtable suffragist Mrs Mabel St Clair Stobart, which had done good service during the Balkan War in 1912. There was also the Women's Hospital Corps, raised by Dr Flora Murray and Louisa Garrett Anderson in September 1914. All of these units offered their services, voluntarily and freely, to the War Office but the reaction they all received is typified by that expressed directly to Edinburgh surgeon Elsie Inglis, founder of another early all-female unit, the Scottish Women's Hospitals, when she was granted a meeting at Whitehall in August 1914. After explaining her proposal she was told by the official, 'My good lady, go home and sit still – no petticoats here.'

Only one women's unit was accepted by the War Office in 1914, the Almeric Paget Military Massage Corps, which offered fifty trained masseuses for work among the wounded in the United Kingdom. The key had been that Mrs Paget did not press for her Corps to serve abroad immediately (a detachment was sent to France in 1917). Scorned, yet undaunted, the other women's voluntary aid units who did wish to serve abroad

Dr Elsie Inglis,
founder of
the Scottish
Women's
Hospitals.
(IWM Q 68949A)

had many well-connected and persuasive ladies within their membership; after negotiations with diplomats and the military of Britain's foreign allies they were welcome to support troops in Belgium, France and Serbia.

After arrangement with the Belgian Army the first troop of six FANYs left for France on 27 October 1914 with three nurses, two orderlies and only £12 of corps funds in the bank. Their first base and 'hospital' was the redundant Lamarck convent school on the Rue de la Rivière, Paris with the magnificent east window of Notre Dame facing their yard. The school was decayed and dirty, the stench of the latrines was appalling and inside were about forty desperately ill men on plank beds. Always resourceful and dedicated to the challenge before them, the FANYs appealed to friends and acquaintances at home to send sheets,

One of the largest
detachments of
FANYs despatched
to France in 1914.

pillowcases, bedspreads and soft pillows. The British Red Cross also helped by supplying narrow spring beds with good mattresses. Lamarck Hospital soon had a hundred good beds and treated more than four thousand patients between 1914 and 1916, many of them brought to the doors in ambulances driven by FANY drivers.

The FANY corps ran a number of field hospitals, drove ambulances, operated a motor bath providing 250 baths a day, and disinfected soldiers' clothes; they also set up soup kitchens and troop canteens often under highly dangerous conditions across the Western Front but still they remained a comparatively small unit. In August 1918 there were just 120 FANYs serving in France but their contribution and bravery was outstanding. By the time of the Armistice, among their membership they could claim seventeen British Military Medals, a Legion d'Honneur and twenty-seven Croix de Guerre.

Another unit welcomed by the Belgian Army was a small flying ambulance corps raised by Dr Hector Munro. A feminist sympathiser, he included four women in his team: one Scottish girl named Mairi

Two FANYs removing a stretcher case from their ambulance to hospital.

Badge of the First Aid Nursing Yeomanry.

Five FANY drivers,
with their own
fur coats, sent by
special request
from their families
at home, Calais,
January 1917.
(IWM Q 4669)

Elsie Knocker and
Mairi Chisholm –
the 'Women of
Pervyse', July 1917.

Chisholm, Lady Dorothy Fielding and Elsie Knocker (later Baroness T'Serclaes) from England, and an American, Mrs Helen Gleason. Chisholm and Knocker became close friends – both were dedicated to their cause and both were keen motorcyclists. For the first two months Mairi drove ambulances (often under fire over increasingly difficult terrain) while Elsie, a trained nurse, tended to the wounded. In November 1914 they established a small first aid post close to the front line in the ruined Belgian village of Pervyse, north of Ypres. Their brave deeds soon reached the press and they became simply known as 'Women of Pervyse". Despite being bombed out on two occasions and wounded, they carried on and maintained first aid posts near the front line for the majority of the war. Honoured by the award of the Star of the Order of Leopold personally by King Albert of Belgium, they were later both awarded the British Military Medal.

Deeds of heroism by Red Cross women always made popular features in the press, such as this cover story from *The War Budget*, September 1915.

Mrs Mabel St Clair Stobart's Women's Sick and Wounded Convoy Corps was also welcomed by the Belgian Army and she helped establish field hospitals in France and Flanders for the St John Ambulance in 1914. Mrs St Clair Stobart was captured by the Germans at Antwerp and accused of being a spy and threatened with execution by firing squad. Released and repatriated she answered the appeal for medical assistance in the Serbian campaign. Her pre-war experience in the Balkans made her the obvious candidate to lead the Third Serbian Relief Fund unit and established their headquarters at Kragujevac in April 1915.

There had been a medical presence in Kragujevac since August 1914 in the form of the St John Ambulance unit of thirty-six women raised by Mabel Grouitch. Among this unit was Flora Sandes who went on to join the Serbian Red Cross and worked in an ambulance for the Second Infantry Regiment of the Serbian Army. Separated from her unit during the retreat to Albania she joined a Serbian regiment rather than risk being taken for a spy; with this act she became the only known British woman to legitimately join and serve in a fighting unit during the First World War. Injured in hand-to-hand combat during the advance on Bitola, she was

A Red Cross Heroine

Sergeant Major
Flora Sandes chats
to a Serbian officer
on a street corner,
Salonika, Greece.
(IWM Q 32704)

Sergeant Major Flora Sandes chats to a Serbian officer on a street corner, Salonika, Greece. (IWM Q 32704)

subsequently awarded the Order of Kara George and became a legend in
the Serbian Army, who dubbed her 'Our Joan of Arc'. Flora published her
autobiography, *An English Woman-Sergeant in the Serbian Army*, in 1916 to help
her raise funds for the Serbian Army.

Mrs St Clair Stobart led her 'Flying Field Hospital Column' on
horseback. In September 1915 she was appointed Commander of Column,
First Serbian English Field Hospital. In October 1915 the Serbian Army was
facing defeat and was forced to undertake a horrendous retreat across the
mountains of Albania to find sanctuary in Italy and Corfu. Many lives were
lost but Mabel St Clair Stobart and her ambulance column brought succour
to many as she and her column travelled with them through liquefied mud
and bitter snow and frost, suffering hunger and treating frostbite, gangrene
and typhus.

Elsie Inglis and her Scottish Women's Hospitals also found a placement with the Serbian Army, deployed to northern Serbia in January 1915. By 1918 there were fourteen such units, working with each of the Allied armies with the ludicrous exception of the British. Inglis was taken prisoner of war in Serbia in 1915. After repatriation she immediately joined another unit and served in Russia. Evacuated after the Revolution, she died the day after her return home to Newcastle in November 1917.

The Women's Hospital Corps went on to establish military hospitals for the French Army in Paris and Wimereux but later, in the light of the high-profile achievements of the other women's aid units the War Office magnanimously allowed the WHC to establish a military hospital staffed entirely by women, from chief surgeon to orderlies, on Endell Street, London.

Mrs Mabel
St Clair Stobart.
(IWM Q 69129)

It was a small gain but the first of many. The women's units of the later years of the First World War are direct descendants of the women's units established in 1914; they represent what these early pioneers of women's service fought, and in some cases, died for – the right of women to serve.

A FANY
ambulance driver
being decorated
by General Plumer
for bravery during
air raids,
Blendeques,
France, July 1918.
(IWM Q6791)

FRANCE
ITALY
MALTA
GIBRA~~L~~
SALON

ECYPT
MESOPOTAMIA
HOLLAND
SWITZERLAND
RUSSIA

V.A.D.

NURSING MEMBERS , COOKS, KITCHEN·MAIDS,
CLERKS , HOUSE·MAIDS . WARD·MAIDS,
LAUNDRESSES, MOTOR·DRIVERS. ETC:

ARE URGENTLY NEEDED

APPLICATION TO BE MADE TO

NURSING SERVICES

THE Queen Alexandra's Imperial Military Nursing Service (QAIMNS), named in honour of HM Queen Alexandra, replaced the Army Nursing Service by Royal Warrant on 27 March 1902; by the same decree Queen Alexandra's Royal Naval Nursing Service and the Indian Nursing Service were created and a QAIMNS Reserve soon followed. The Territorial Force Nursing Service (TFNS) was formed as part of the Haldane Reforms of the British Army in 1908 from women volunteers, all of whom had qualified and served as nurses in civilian life. It would soon boast a membership of over three thousand. Their role was originally intended to be the staff for the twenty-three War Office controlled Territorial Hospitals that were to be established across the country in pre-identified locations in the event of war.

The army saw no need to recruit and maintain a large cadre of military nurses in peacetime so when war was declared in 1914 the QAIMNS could not claim any membership like the TFNS; there were only 297 regular members. The criteria for recruitment did not help either: rules for appointment in the QAIMNS were strict; candidates had to be over twenty-five, single and be of a high social status. Most girls from this social group were married by twenty-five, so any girl joining must have been dedicated to make this job a career for life. During the war, as the casualties mounted and the pressure for more QA nurses grew, the rules had to be relaxed and more allowed to join. By the end of the war there were over ten thousand nurses serving in the various branches of the British military nursing services.

By far the greatest number of uniformed nurses during the First World War were those who had volunteered and had been trained by the British Red Cross Society or St John Ambulance. After the creation of the Territorial Force in 1908, the War Office issued its 'Scheme for the Organisation of Voluntary Aid in England and Wales' in the following year. The War Office had recognised that in the event of a major European war existing medical arrangements for its armed forces would be wholly inadequate. Some form of supplementary aid would be required, in addition to the Territorial Force Medical Service, to provide transport and care for returned wounded.

Opposite:
Voluntary Aid Detachment recruitment poster, c. 1915. The international work of the Joint War Organisation is well demonstrated by the many countries listed upon it.

A Sister of Queen
Alexandra's
Imperial Military
Nursing Service
(right) and a
Matron of the
Territorial Force
Nursing Service,
c. 1918.
(IWM Q 30364)

The Red Cross and St John Ambulance
(although at that time working as separate
voluntary aid societies) immediately began to
establish Voluntary Aid Detachments (VADs)
to recruit and train local volunteers for the
task. There were no mixed detachments. Male
detachments were the most difficult to recruit
because they required fifty-six volunteers,
headed by a Commandant, with a Medical
Officer, Quartermaster and Honorary
Secretary, Pharmacist and four sections, each
comprising a Section Leader and twelve men.

A women's detachment of twenty-four
was far simpler. Led by a Commandant and
Lady Superintendent (a trained nurse) the
detachment comprised four sections, each with
a Section Leader and four women, or two
sections each with one Section Leader and nine
women. Within its ranks, each female
detachment had to include four proficient cooks.

To become full and proficient members of their Voluntary Aid
Detachment, girls were expected to train for and pass examinations in both
first aid and nursing. The VAD (a term applied to all serving in the VAD

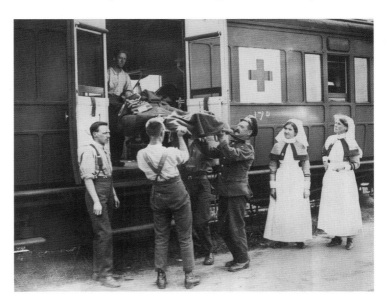

British Army
Nurses stand
ready to attend
casualties from
the Battle of
Passchendaele,
France, 1917.
(IWM CO 1801)

system, but more especially to the nurses) was to 'regard herself as part of the Medical Organisation of the Territorial Force, available to serve in the event of war'.

By the outbreak of war Voluntary Aid Detachments had been established across the country, personnel had been trained, and many had staged exercises, setting up emergency hospitals in public halls, schools, tents and even cricket pavilions. In August 1914 there were some nine thousand VAD members (by 1918 there were twenty-three thousand nurses and eighteen thousand nursing orderlies). There were two classes of VAD volunteer. The first class was termed 'mobile' – these nurses were to make themselves available for service anywhere, and indeed many served with great distinction in theatres of war all over the world. They were not always miles behind the lines – many were involved in the removal of troops under fire and on occasion their hospitals suffered air raids, such as at Étaples, which was

Right: Medallion worn on the right of the tippet by members of the Territorital Force Nursing Service.

Below: Voluntary Aid Detachment (Walsingham), Norfolk Branch, British Red Cross Society, 1914.

Postcard of nurses 'in the field': an illustration based on a textbook picture (including the cricket pavilion converted to an operating theatre), sold to raise money for the Red Cross Fund in 1914–15.

Photographed on 2 June 1918, nurses survey the damage sustained during air raids on the Hospital Area, Étaples, after the bombing of 30–31 May 1918. In total, about two hundred nurses from British military nursing services died while serving during the First World War. (IWM Q 11539)

bombed on the night of 30–31 May 1918. One ward received a direct hit and was blown to pieces, six wards were reduced to ruins, and three more were severely damaged. Sister Baines, four orderlies, and eleven patients were killed outright, whilst two doctors, five sisters, and many orderlies and patients were wounded.

VAD ambulance
drivers, Étaples,
June 1917.
(IWM Q 2438)

An Order of
St John VAD nurse
armband, worn
on the right arm,
sometimes in
conjunction with
a Red Cross
'protection'
brassard on
the left.

The largest component of the VAD system were those classified 'immobile' – the nurses who registered to serve only in areas local to them in the Auxiliary War Hospitals (also known as 'VAD Hospitals' and 'Red Cross Hospitals').

At the outbreak of war, public meetings were held across the country to ascertain which public buildings and houses were available for conversion to Auxiliary War Hospitals. In most cases a large local house or the rectory proved to be the most practical place in which to open a hospital, although hospital 'annexes' were opened in public buildings or other houses when returning casualties overwhelmed the bed space available.

In the opening months of the war the Red Cross and the Order of St John were brought together in the Joint War Committee, with the internationally recognised symbol and name of the Red Cross taking precedence. Wartime recruitment of VADs was never a problem. Girls wishing to nurse had to be 'presentable' and had to provide a reference or recommendation from a local doctor, priest or magistrate. They also had to be able to give time to their duties on a regular basis. In 1915, with the introduction of the 'General Service' section of the VAD, there was a

British Red Cross
Society and Order
of St John Joint
War Organisation
VAD driver's badge
worn on the left
sleeve just above
the cuff. This
particular example
was worn by Miss
A. Worthington-
Wilmer
throughout her
service on
ambulance convoys
in France, 1915–19.

St John nurses
at Étaples, France,
June 1917.
(IWM Q 2520)

wide variety of duties for girls of most abilities, so most could find a place –
as a cook or laundress, a clerk, typist, telephonist, driver, chauffeur, or as a
VAD nurse.

The premier position of VAD nurse was often the preserve of the young
ladies from local middle- and upper-class families who could afford to give
the time, pay for the lectures
and had £1 19s 2½d to buy a
uniform (although later in the
war local VAD units did have
funds to issue uniforms, or at
least replace worn out aprons,
collars and cuffs). Officially,
VAD nursing members had to
be twenty-three to thirty-eight
years old to serve in military
hospitals but if girls looked old
enough and were keen enough
they would get in. Girls as
young as seventeen became
VADs, especially in the
provincial Auxiliary War
Hospitals. They were
appointed on two weeks'
probation, and if they were
found to be suitable, they

Within days of the
outbreak of war
posters like this
one went up all
over Britain. High
on the agenda was
the desire to raise
Auxiliary War
Hospitals in the
local area, hence
they were often
run under the
auspices of the
British Red Cross
Society.

WAR!

URGENT PUBLIC MEETING.

A

PUBLIC MEETING

UNDER THE AUSPICES OF THE

Swaffham Branch of the British

RED CROSS SOCIETY

WILL BE HELD IN THE

Assembly Rooms,

ON THURSDAY NEXT

(AUGUST 6th.) AT 8 O'CLOCK.

CHAIRMAN–MR. G. A. WALKER.

The matters to be considered are of vital importance.

ALL ARE INVITED TO ATTEND.

would be expected to serve for up to three months, and many served for much longer. The engagement of VAD members could be terminated if 'at any time they were found unfit in any respect for service'.

Most of the hospitals in the country had a 'family' atmosphere, with the owner of the house or his wife as Commandant of the detachment, and VADs drawn from its domestic staff and local girls. The care supplied was directed by a Medical Officer (often a local doctor) and the Superintendent (a trained nurse). In the early years of the war many of these professionals provided their services free of charge, and some did so throughout the war, but payments were allowed, with a Medical Officer drawing £1 a day. Matrons, sisters-in-charge and ward sisters were paid one guinea (£1 1s) a week, and staff nurses (with two years' training) £40 a year. The VAD nurses who served part-time in their local hospital were

One of the Best !

The 'Romance of the Red Cross' throughout the war was reflected in all manner of memorabilia, from china goods and souvenir badges to postcards like this one.

Staff of the Auxiliary War Hospital, Melton Lodge, Great Yarmouth, Norfolk, 1917.

Red Cross and St John outfits offered for supply by Hussey & Co. in 1917.

unpaid, but expenses for board and lodging, laundry (up to a limit of 2s 6d) and travel to and from the hospital could be claimed. There was also a Compassionate Fund, which assisted sick or injured VAD personnel.

The term 'nurse' for the VADs was one which some members of the public objected to as VADS were 'not fully trained', so the Joint War Committee took pains to publish the following clarification and endorsement of the VADs:

> There is not, and never has been, any reasonable doubt as to what constitutes a fully trained nurse… In every large hospital there is a matron, and there are sisters, staff nurses and probationers. The matron and sisters are addressed by their titles, but staff nurses and probationers are alike addressed as 'Nurse'. A probationer of only one day's standing would consequently be called, for example, 'Nurse Jones'… It was, therefore, in accordance with the usual practice that a VAD member engaged in the nursing department of any hospital should be called 'Nurse'.

Role and rank were defined by the colour of indoor uniforms. Commandants wore a bright scarlet dress, quartermasters grey, cooks pale brown and the

nurses, the iconic pale blue dress. All were expected to have the correct clean white headgear, and starched detachable collars and cuffs. The nurses' aprons were not issued with a red cross on the breast, so they had make their own but because there were no guidelines for the dimensions of the cross, you will rarely see any two that are quite alike. To appear more experienced, young nurses quickly put their aprons through the wash a few times so that the red cross grew lighter, while some VADs were not above using a bleach to 'pink' their cross. Legs were clad in black stockings, with skirts at ankle-length, worn with everyday boots or shoes.

Outdoor dress for nurses consisted of a long, single-breasted greatcoat and a distinctive cloth hat with a metal Red Cross badge. A Commandant

Nurse Sybil Parker,
VAD, 1914.

Studio portrait of a VAD nurse in her outdoor uniform, 1914.

Below:
Red Cross 'protection' brassard, worn on the left arm (1914). It was named so because if there was an invasion the person authorised to wear this armband was entitled to the international protection accorded to Red Cross personnel.

wore a smart two-piece jacket and skirt, blouse with collar and tie, their insignia of rank displayed on the cuffs, topped by a fine black or dark navy straw or felt hat with a ribbon and badge. In the early years of the war VADs were encouraged to wear Red Cross 'brassards' (armbands) and to carry their 'identity and authority to

wear' card to identify them as Red Cross workers. In theory, this gave them the protection of the Red Cross in the event of an invasion. The card and armband were also to be carried while wearing civilian clothes in the event of emergency (especially air raids), to show that they had been trained in first aid.

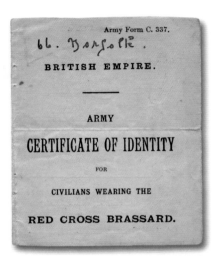

Reverse of the Red Cross armband, showing endorsement stamps from the wearer's Voluntary Aid Detachment with brassard number stamped in the centre and Army Medical Service dated across the centre.

To provide 24-hour cover, VADs worked shifts, girls arriving on foot, riding bicycles or being dropped off by pony and cart. Although they may have been assigned certain core duties, no two days would be quite the same for a VAD. Convalescent men were allocated to the hospitals from two sources. Some would be despatched on trains or by ambulance after treatment in the main county or district War Hospital. Some would come almost direct from France having passed

Just as important as the armband was the certificate of identity to go with it, which would record the name, nationality, age and distinguishing features of the holder as well as the brassard number and signatures of the cardholder and officer representing the issuing authority.

through continental field hospitals with 'Blighty wounds' which, if they only required basic treatment and convalescence, could mean that men were sent directly to an Auxiliary War Hospital, many still in their muddy and bloody uniforms.

A telegram would be sent to the hospital Commandant to alert her of the arrival of fresh wounded, and if they were not delivered by ambulance, a reception committee would have to be despatched to the local railway station. In many rural areas there were no ambulances, and hastily converted delivery vehicles and private cars were used, along with a motley collection of wheelchairs and hand-drawn carriages, with VAD escorts for the walking wounded.

At the hospital, the VADs and male orderlies would assist the storekeeper in exchanging khaki for the flannel 'hospital blue' uniform of jacket and trousers, white shirt and red tie worn with the soldier's own cap and boots for trips out of doors (slippers being issued for inside

The badge of the BRCS & Order of St John Joint War Organisation.

Auxiliary War Hospitals would be warned of the impending arrival of wounded for their care by telegram.

Our Hospital A B C – just one of numerous amusing books and cartoons that reflected the trials, tribulations and life of VAD nurses with good humour and affection.

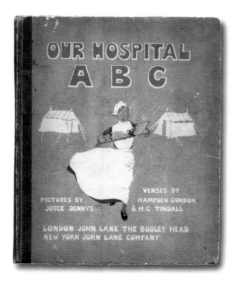

wear). The soft and shapeless 'blues' aided the identification of any wandering serviceman who had slipped out, perhaps for a strictly forbidden pint! Times of blues shortage, or particularly heavy numbers of returning wounded, can be noted in old photographs, with convalescent troops still wearing their khaki uniforms.

A typical day began with nurses assisting those patients marked 'Up' to rise, shave, wash and dress before breakfast. Some patients would be marked 'Up from and to', the specific times of day set by the Medical Officer (MO). Patients ordered 'bed rest' would be made to look presentable for the MO's inspection rounds. The nurses would follow the MO, Commandant and Lady Superintendent during this inspection. Once the MO's rounds were over, the VAD nurses would assist the MO and Lady Superintendent in changing dressings. Young VADs were daily confronted with sights that would haunt their dreams for the rest of their lives. One former nurse recalled a young soldier whose head was completely swathed in a heavy bandage. As she slowly unwound the bandage she wondered if there could actually be a head left inside its folds.

Throughout the day, bedpans and sputum cups had to be supplied and emptied, and Nelson's inhalers used to clear congestion on the lungs. The incapable would be fed, and those learning to walk again helped onto crutches or supported. To occupy convalescent troops most wards had been gifted a host of comforts, such as gramophones, books and magazines. Crafts such as rag rug making and embroidery were taught to the bed-bound. Many VADs patiently helped the wounded to write home, took dictation or read letters to the blinded, always doing their best to remain cheerful. There were regular teas and concerts held at the hospitals to help keep up morale or help to raise funds. The VADs would help the convalescent troops to make decorations, such as paper link chains and Chinese lanterns. If there

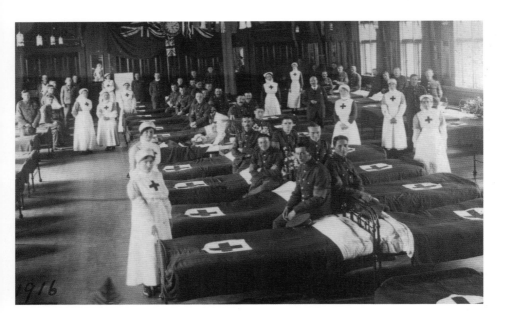

was a sports element, such as cricket, involved in an event, the convalescent soldier might bat while a local Boy Scout, recruited by the nurses, would be the soldier's runner.

Many VADs kept autograph books in which their patients were encouraged not just to write a message or rhyme but to draw a picture of, say, his cap badge, to paint or draw his vision of home, happy memories, flowers, birds or cartoons. A few of these books have survived as deeply

Forester's Hall annexe for the Towers Auxiliary War Hospital, Downham Market, Norfolk (1916).

VAD Nurses at work in a ward at the Henham Hall Auxiliary War Hospital, Suffolk (1915).

VAD Nurses and
convalescent
soldiers at
Dereham Auxiliary
War Hospital,
Norfolk, 1915.

moving records of the thoughts and feelings of the thousands of servicemen
from all over the world who were treated in Britain's Auxiliary War Hospitals
during the First World War.

Nurses' memento
books from
Auxiliary War
Hospitals at
Binefield House
in Oxted, Surrey,
and Attleborough,
Norfolk.

A HEROINE IN A LEAGUE OF HER OWN

Edith Louisa Cavell (1865–1915), Britain's greatest heroine of the First World War, shall forever be associated with the symbol and ethos of the Red Cross. Born at Swardeston in Norfolk and trained as a nurse at Fountains Fever Hospital in Lower Tooting and the London Hospital, Edith was appointed Matron of the École Belge d'Infirmières Diplômées at Brussels in 1907. Despite Belgium being in imminent danger of invasion she returned there from a holiday in England in August 1914. Edith impressed on her nurses that their first duty was to care for the wounded irrespective of nationality. In the autumn of 1914, two bedraggled and wounded British soldiers were sheltered by Edith for two weeks; more followed and soon an escape route to neutral territory in Holland was established. Edith's motives were simple: the protection, concealment and the smuggling away of hunted men constituted as much a humanitarian act as tending to the sick and wounded. The secret escape organisation lasted for almost a year, until a Belgian collaborator betrayed the group and Edith was arrested.

One of many variations of tribute cards produced in memory of Edith Cavell.

Tried and found guilty of 'conducting soldiers to the Enemy' and despite international appeals for clemency Edith was executed by firing squad on 12 October 1915 at the *Tir Nationale* (National Rifle Range). The night before her execution she was attended by Chaplain Stirling Gahan. His account recalls Edith wished all her friends to know that she willingly gave her life for her country and said:

> I have seen death so often that it is not fearful or strange to me, and this I would say, standing as I do in view of God and Eternity. I realise patriotism is not enough. I must have no hatred or bitterness against anyone.

The 'Murder' or 'Martyrdom' of 'Nurse' Cavell (A forty-nine-year-old Matron clearly did not have the same media appeal as the younger and pretty sounding 'Nurse') became a cause célèbre and soon her image and story appeared on posters, papers, magazines, postcards, in memoriam cards and all manner of souvenirs from badges to commemorative china. After the Armistice Edith's body was exhumed and returned to England to be given a full honours funeral; via Westminster Abbey, Edith Cavell was finally laid to rest at Life's Green outside Norwich Cathedral on 15 May 1919.

MUNITIONETTES AND WOMEN WAR WORKERS

THE MEN who had left their jobs on 'civvy street' to serve in the forces left a huge gap in the workforce. Many ladies had taken over the vacancies to carry out simple clerking and shop work in local businesses, factory work (such as boot making or tinned foods) and light agricultural work (such as fruit picking or helping with the grain harvest) since August 1914. However, in most of these areas employers took on female staff with the strict understanding that it was only a stop gap measure and that when the man returned he would be able to have his job back; and most ladies were quite happy with the arrangement – it was 'the patriotic thing to do'.

There was also a small but significant number of Women's Police Volunteers (WPV). Although some chief constables refused to endorse their cards of authority a number of forces were grateful to them, especially in areas where the WPV would be willing to patrol for 'camp followers' or prostitutes around army camps. For this work Grantham Constabulary swore in Mrs Edith Smith as the first official policewoman with full powers of arrest in 1915.

There was, however a potential army of women who wanted to do something for the war effort but were simply not being utilised. The National Union of Women's Suffrage Societies had suspended its militant action to allow for concentration on the war effort, so when they felt they were not being used effectively the country could expect these women would soon find a way of voicing their demands. On 17 March 1915 the Board of Trade issued an appeal to women to register for 'war service' work at their local Labour Exchange. Significantly the appeal pointed out that they could be 'required for paid employment of any kind – industrial, agricultural or clerical'. And they went further still: 'Women are wanted at once in farm work, dairy work, brush making, leather stitching, clothing machinery and light machining for armaments.' After the first week of the announcement over twenty-thousand registrations were received but the take-up by employers was slow and in the immediate aftermath of the appeal many women felt that their hopes had been raised unnecessarily and their

In massive contrast to the Women of Britain say-Go! poster of 1914, the munitions worker depicted on this poster from around 1917 still bids farewell to her uniformed husband, but this girl is ready to do her bit too. (IWM PST 3283)

Women war workers feed the charcoal kilns used for purifying sugar at a sugar refinery in Scotland. (IWM Q 28351)

time wasted. But further events in 1915 were to truly galvanise action for getting women into war work.

This sea change began with the 'Shells Scandal' of 1915 after the publication of the startling revelation that in the opinion of Sir John French (the British Commander-in-Chief) a shortage of munitions led directly to the failure of the British offensive at Neuve Chapelle in March 1915. The Liberal Chancellor David Lloyd George fervently believed radical improvements were required in the munitions industry if Britain was going to carry on a prolonged war against Germany. The 'Shells Scandal' became a key factor in the fall of the Liberal Government in May 1915 and the establishment of a new coalition in which the new Ministry of Munitions was created under Lloyd George. The 'Women's March Through London' was staged on 21 July 1915. Some thirty-thousand women marched through the capital under the banner, 'We Demand the Right to Serve.' The pressure was on and as a direct result of the scandal munitions work was expanded and after the march far more women were going to do their bit too!

Women substituting men in industries other than munitions came under the aegis of The Factory Department of the Home Office. With the Board of Trade now actively seeking placements, thousands of women went to work in factories and businesses; many local firms also recruited women under their own initiatives. Soon women were employed in such diverse industries as rubber moulding, manufacturing (products included children's shoes, concrete, golden syrup, glucose, mustard, linoleum, soap, hats and bread), pottery, piano making, oil seed crushing and working in flour mills. Women's labour also became more mobile in unprecedented ways – single women could move from a locality where employment was slack to another where her labour was in demand. One of the biggest moves of women en masse came from the east coast of Scotland, where the fisher girls were suffering from a slump in the herring trade and were moved to the jute mills in Dundee. This new mobility was to have the most profound effect on individual women who for the first time gained a feeling of freedom, choice and a sense of adventure embarking on employment, often for the first time.

The employment of women did not occur without opposition; there were some petty instances where some men refused to work with women. This seems to have been particularly prevalent on the tramways and amongst licensed vehicle workers such as taxi drivers. Tramway Workers made a formal resolution in May 1915 claiming that to employ women on the tramways was a dangerous proposal and made resolutions that no women should be employed while it was possible to obtain men – although by the end of 1915 half the Manchester tram conductors were women. There were also women tram drivers to be found around Britain but still petty regulations denied the women equal pay or the same rights as their male counterparts; for example, women tram drivers were not always permitted to turn round the trolley, thus denying them war bonuses which, instead, would be paid to the male driver who would perform this extra task. Even in 1917 the General Secretary of the London and Provincial Union of Licensed Vehicle Workers wrote to the Home Secretary warning of his Executive Council's concerns for 'serious consequences' (such as strikes) and warning of the accidents that would 'inevitably' occur if women were allowed to drive licensed vehicles.

Far more women were taken onto the national workforce in 1916 after the introduction of conscription saw thousands more men leave their places of work to serve in the forces. More women were becoming drivers of horse-drawn delivery carts as well as motorised vehicles and vans. Many upper-class women could already drive, and a number of them that owned their own cars drove for the Royal Automobile Club Owner-Drivers' War Service Corps. For those who had never driven cars or motorbikes, garages offered tuition, as did some wartime organisations. In early 1916 the Metropolitan Asylums Board became the

A girl in trousers and overalls tugs at the handle of a glucose press in a Lancaster glucose mill. (IWM Q 28218)

first major public body to employ female drivers. Like so many times before, the women proved themselves perfectly competent and by July 1916 the London County Council Ambulance Corps was run entirely by women, many of them working shifts of twelve to thirteen hours a day; but they were paid well at £2 5s 0d per week with uniform and lodging at 'cosy quarters near Russell Square'. Many of the lingering dissenting voices were quieted by the pressure to keep the country running and by the National Service Scheme of early 1917, which covered all aspects of civilian and non-combative employment. The number of omnibus conductresses rose from a token few in 1916 to about 2,500 in early 1917; women also became omnibus drivers in the provinces. Many more women were employed upon the railways, not just in clerical positions but as porters, ticket collectors, in signal boxes and as lamp girls; women went to work with the platelayers of the railway bed, shifting and raking ballast while many others went into the engine sheds and donned their overalls to help maintain, clean and prepare engines and carriages. Even the National Union of Railwaymen and Amalgamated Association of Tramway and Vehicle Workers opened their membership to women. By 1918 more than 65,000 women were employed on Britain's railways.

Between 1916 and 1918 unprecedented numbers of women took on occupations that in pre-war Britain would have been unimaginable to Edwardian society, working as chimney sweeps, road sweepers, bicycle messengers, park keepers, gardeners (some of them in the Royal Gardens at Kew), funeral directors, bill-posters, window cleaners and pushing milk carts. Some women entered into labour-intensive areas, working as bricklayers, coal heavers, in steel yards and gravel pits, in breweries, foundries, and even stoking the fire in gasworks.

Women cleaners employed by the Lancashire and Yorkshire Railway at Low Moor engine shed near Bradford, 23 March 1917.

One of them recalled:

> We were hardy sorts but many was the time that a girl would be affected by the gas, the remedy being to walk them up and down outside in the fresh air then get them to drink a bottle of Guinness.

By 1918 women were working in shipyards among the riveters, taking the place of boys heating and conveying the rivets to the men who drove them home. They were working in the blacksmith's forge, they red-leaded iron work and did their share of the painting. All over the shipyard women could be found working the planing machines in the joiner's shop, operating screwing and boring machines, driving electric cranes and winches, shifting scrap iron, carrying balks of timbers and even helping to unpack big cases of machine parts or unloading bars of iron from railway wagons – causing more than one commentator to admit their surprise at how the women were being employed, and their clear ability and confidence at doing the job in hand.

Proud to be 'doing the rounds' – Violet Jackson, postwoman, 1917.

Most famous of the women workers of the First World War were those employed in the munitions factories, but few people realise that the term 'munitions' did not just refer to the manufacture of shells but a whole host of operations as diverse as pulling flax crops to manufacturing wooden boxes for military purposes, and even working in the various stages of aircraft manufacture. Broadly speaking if it involved 'feeding the guns' of the war effort it could be titled munitions work – so a girl could have been involved in munitions throughout the war without ever having touched a gun shell!

That said, the largest number of women employed in munitions work were working in the manufacture of explosives, gun shells, small arms ammunitions and shell-filling factories. Initially, this dangerous and hard manual work was deemed as 'quite unsuitable' for women but such opinions were very out of touch; in 1914 thousands of women were already working in engineering and munitions. After the creation of the Ministry of Munitions in 1915 more and more women were recruited to feed the guns and all women employed within this sphere would come under the aegis of the Ministry of Munitions. Existing munitions factories were enlarged and a new build scheme saw super factories of an unprecedented size built and a massive workforce employed in the

manufacture of explosives and gun shells. Many businesses across the country were adapted for various single stages of shell production (such as manufacturing fuses, shell cases or ammunition boxes) but most explosives were produced at the National Explosives Factories such as NEF Pembrey in Carmarthenshire, Wales, and Silvertown, West Ham, which produced TNT. The explosives would then be moved by train to a 'filling factory' – a munitions factory that specialised in filling the shells.

Glasgow Corporation tram driver and conductor, 1918. (IWM Q 28389)

A woman parcel truck driver of the Great Eastern Railway Company driving a battery-powered rail parcel truck in 1918. She is wearing her own patterned stockings and clasp shoes with her uniform. (IWM Q 27983)

The greatest of all the new munitions works was His Majesty's Factory, Gretna, adjacent to the Solway Firth. Construction work began in November 1915 and production of munitions began in April 1916. The completed site occupied an area stretching some 12 miles from Mossband in the east to Dornock and Eastriggs in the west and consisted of four massive production sites, two townships for workers, and even had its own telephone exchange, coal-fired power station, water supply with reservoir, filtration system and water pumping stations and a light railway network with 125 miles of track and thirty-four railway engines. At its peak output Gretna produced 800 tons of Cordite RDB a week (nicknamed 'devil's porridge') and by 1917 employed a predominantly female workforce (11,576 women and 5,066 men.)

Two female bag fillers use two short poles to assist a female coke heaver as she hoists a large sack of coke onto her back, 1918. (IWM Q 30859)

37

Gauging shells at Royal Shell Factory 3 at Woolwich Arsenal, May 1918. (IWM Q 27870)

So, who were the munitions girls? Class was certainly a factor: 'nice' girls from middle- and upper-class families tended to be guided towards nursing organisations or women's services, whereas the munitions girls were predominantly from domestic service backgrounds with a liberal smattering of shop assistants, laundry workers and clerks and others from similar working- and lower-middle-class backgrounds. Requirements were similar to those of any other occupation in this employment sector – basic education and physical fitness to do the job was enough. The days were long, many factories working 24 hours a day with girls working twelve-hour shifts (typically 6am to 6pm and vice versa for the next shift). Although there were great disputes over the inequality of wages – men were paid an average £4 6s 6d, whereas women only received £2 2s 4d a week – most girls were quite happy because the wages were higher than they were accustomed to before the war.

Cartoonist Fred Spurgin depicts a very glamorous Munitionette, c. 1915.

YOU SHOULD SEE HOW THE
GIRLS FILL THEM!

But these girls had serious and often dangerous work to do. By the middle of the war some 75,000 women were employed in the munitions industry and were literally producing millions of shells and small arms ammunition every year. In each major filling factory there would be separate work 'departments' or 'groups' (for example, one area makes detonators, primers and fuzes; another fills the fuzes; another blends the gunpowder for time fuzes, while another fills the brass shell cases with cordite). These departments would be situated at geographically different areas but still within the designated 'danger area' of the factory, hence the light railway to run between them.

Outside the danger area would be located the administration and pay offices, machinery workshops, a medical centre, canteens (on sites like Gretna there would be as many as forty canteens), changing rooms and search rooms where the workers would be checked for 'contraband' such as matches and tobacco.

The girls would be expected to come to work in 'working clothes' but would typically be issued a pair of wooden soled clogs (sparks could be caused by metal cleats or 'blakies', and studded or even plain leather-soled boots are not a good idea when working with explosives). In the most critical areas the girls wore fabric slippers or even rubber gumboots. All would be issued the relevant pattern of 'National Shell Overall', which comprised a drawstring or elasticated cap and a flame retardant canvas or cotton twill overall with a belted waist. Soon numbered brooch and button fitted badges were issued to the workers with an entitlement

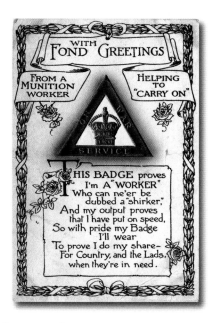

card. These had to be carried at all times along with their general issue identity cards, to show that the worker was entitled to be in the factory – although it must be noted that these badges (or indeed any metal item) were prohibited in the danger areas. Initially many of the factories not owned by

A charming greetings card from a munitions worker, 1916.

Women war workers finishing small arms cartridges in the Small Arms Cartridge Factory (3) at Woolwich Arsenal, May 1918. (IWM Q 27880)

the Ministry of Munitions made their own identity badges but by 1915 the officially issued 'On War Service' badges were standard. Girls also took to wearing 'sweetheart' brooches bearing the regimental badge of their 'boy in khaki' in the centre front of their collars.

The dangers many of these girls were exposed to were very real; stringent precautions against sparks and the rules prohibiting smoking were founded on practical knowledge and awareness of tragedies in the industry when minor explosions had been caused, killing a number of workers. By far the worst explosion occurred at the Silvertown Munitions Factory on 19 January 1917. Approximately 50 tons of TNT exploded, killing seventy-three people and injuring over 400, causing a shockwave to be felt for miles around, which devastated buildings and property in the local area.

Another danger was from over-exposure to the chemicals in cordite and especially TNT which could turn hair a ginger colour and skin yellow (hence the

Above: One of the Gretna Munitionettes wearing her overalls, complete with trousers – a garment simply not worn by women before the First World War. (Geoff Caulton)

Opposite: Munitionettes filling and sealing shells in a workshop at the National Filling Factory, Banbury, 1918. (IWM Q 70671)

girls became nicknamed 'canaries'). Despite warnings from doctors girls kept on working and after a few serious illnesses and fatalities it became common policy to send batches of the 'canaries' off to coastal resorts to clear their systems.

Because of the nature of work and requirement of mobility the shell overall outfit was soon supplemented with trousers, something no young lady would have been seen wearing on the street before the war. This additional item of clothing was worn as a badge of honour on the street by the munitions girls, who soon acquired the nickname 'Munitionettes'.

With the end of the First World War came the end of the need for most of the munitions girls. They had changed society's attitude to women in so many ways and played a major role in earning women the right to vote. A girl from Dornock Munitions Factory recorded a philosophy that seems to sum up these remarkable women:

This badge showed that the wearer was involved in war work (1916). Many Munitionettes wore this badge with great pride, both in and out of their overalls.

Women war workers of Shop D, Cambridge Scientific Instrument Co., 1918.

> We're all here today, mate Tomorrow – perhaps dead, If fate tumbles on us And blows up our shed. Afraid! Are yer kidding? With money to spend! Years back I wore tatters, Now – silk stockings mi friend! I've bracelets and jewellery, Rings envied by friends, A sergeant to swank with, And something to lend. I drive out in taxis, Do theatres in style. And this is mi verdict – It is jolly worthwhile. Worthwhile, for tomorrow. If I'm blown to the sky, I'll have repaid mi wages in death – and pass by.

ON THE LAND

COUNTY WAR AGRICULTURAL COMMITTEES had existed since the outbreak of war when all County Councils had been requested by the President of the Board of Agriculture and Fisheries to set them up to ascertain the needs of farmers and the best means of assisting them in cultivating their land, training women for farm work and to develop the agricultural resources within each county. Although women had worked on farms in dairies, making butter, keeping poultry, and at harvest time for generations before the war – and more joined them as the men were called up for military service – there were only a few organisations getting women working on the land.

To support the massive demand for horse fodder the Women's Forage Corps was formed by a government initiative in 1915 and was administrated by the Army Service Corps (ASC). There was also the Women's Forestry Corps, operated under the aegis of the Timber Supply Department of the Board of Trade. This unit supplied wood for both paper and industry on the home front and prepared wood for construction work for a variety of theatres of war.

The main organisations for women's employment on the land were the Women's National Land Service Corps (later known simply as Women's Land Corps), the Women's Farm and Garden Union and the Land Service Corps, which had made one of its most important objects the organisation of village women into working gangs under leaders. In late 1916 the President of the Board of Agriculture summed up the mood of the moment: 'The victory or defeat in this great War may be brought about on the cornfields and potato lands of Great Britain.' In December of that same year the wheels were set in motion and the national organisation entitled the Women's Land Army was formally established in 1917 with three sections: agricultural, timber cutting and forage.

A key factor in the development of this new organisation was the transfer of the administration of the growing Women's Institute movement to the Board of Agriculture, thus becoming part of the Women's branch of the Food Production Department. The FPD was a dynamic government organisation created specifically to answer fears that Britain could be reduced to fighting

Opposite:
Women's Forage
Corps workers
feed a hay baler
in 1918.
(IWM Q 30686)

43

A land girl and her working horse, ready to go off to the fields. (IWM Q 30652)

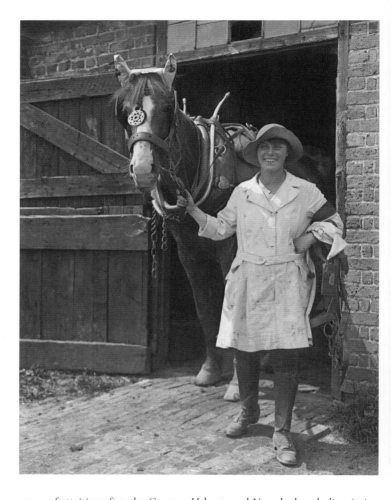

a war of attrition after the German U-boats and Navy had sunk disquieting amounts of merchant shipping and a number of bad winters and subsequent flooding had led to bad harvests. The FPD's remit was to organise and distribute agricultural inputs (such as labour, feed, fertiliser and machinery) to increase output of crops. The FPD officials had a wide range of emergency powers to enforce proper cultivation; for example, they could cross private property, dispossess inefficient tenant farmers and order new land to be ploughed up.

Initially there was scepticism from farmers and from the public in general about the ability of women to 'take the place of a man' on a farm; then there were the questions of billeting, a consideration of 'the loneliness of farm

work' and wages. To address all these concerns the Board of Agriculture set up special sections dealing with training and hostels, county organisation, equipment and publicity materials.

Norfolk Forage Company ASC, Cantley Chaffing Store Staff, c. 1915.

Women's Agriculture Committees were created in every county; county offices were opened and Organising Secretaries appointed, often with very keen and enthusiastic support from two or three Honorary Secretaries; then followed the appointment of the Travelling Inspectors and of Group Leaders in the villages.

Recruitment campaigns were broadcast through the press and staged at open-air rallies, and there was *The Landswoman*, a monthly magazine for both prospective recruits and women already serving. Those wishing to join could volunteer at the rallies or apply for enrolment forms at a post office or employment exchange. Every applicant would have to supply three references obtained from the likes of their employer, their local minister and their doctor, and enrolment would require the signing of a binding contract for either six months or a year's service. They would face a selection panel – some 45,000 young women applied, of whom about 50 per cent were rejected. Miss Meriel Talbot, the Land Army Director, fervently believed, 'We were confident nothing would be more damaging to the whole enterprise than the girl who would not or could not stick it.' About 23,000 were ultimately enrolled; they would then be placed at a farm for training. The time period of training did vary between four to six weeks depending on the stipulation of their local Board or the nature of the work.

The importance of the work of the Land Army was appreciated but there were lingering concerns in some quarters about the girls losing their femininity, not only because of the hard-working nature of their labours but because the land girls wore breeches. These concerns were recognised in the *Land Army Handbook*, which pointed out, 'You are doing a man's work and so you're dressed rather like a man, but remember, just because you wear a smock and breeches you should take care to behave like a British girl who expects chivalry and respect from everyone she meets.' The spirit of change was certainly marked among the girls from the middle class. One lady pointed out in a letter published in her old girls' school magazine: 'You haven't got to ruin your hands, one good nailbrush, one cake of soap, a pair of nail scissors, and a pot of vaseline – I need not tell you how to use them – and the soldiers are sacrificing far more than their hands, aren't they?' The recruiting literature was always keen to point out that as a member of the Land Army people will 'admire your independence and your modesty, your frankness and enthusiasm; show them that an English girl who is working for her country on the land is the best sort of girl'.

Land girls raising their hoes in a salute, 1918. Their smiles, exuberance and vigour reflect the new freedom felt by so many women who, for the first time, had a chance 'to do their bit'.
(IWM Q 30678)

CHAMBERLINS of Norwich

+   +   +

Specialists
and
Makers
of
Uniforms
for
**WOMEN
LAND
WORKERS, &c.**

Red Cross
Outfitters.

Manufacturers
of
**"PEGAMOID"
HEAD-GEAR,**
the Lightest
and most
practical
shield for
Sun or Rain.

The "CROMER."
Thoroughly useful and practical
Uniform for Women working on
the land, or other outdoor occupa-
tion. Adaptable as Breeches or
Trousers. Made of strong cotton
Garbardine Suiting, in Khaki,
Fawn, Brown, Blue-Grey, Navy.

Price 18/11

There were concerns over discipline, since many girls were in high spirits and saw this as one great adventure and a chance for freedom impossible in the years before the war. Letters of complaint and concern were published in both local and national papers of girls failing to wear their overalls at all times, thus revealing their breeches, and of girls going into public houses or staying out of their billets after 9.30pm. More 'effective control' was demanded, as in the request from Lady Mather Jackson, Chairman of the Ladies Committee of Monmouthshire War Agricultural Committee to Land Army Director Miss Talbot, in which she complains that the girls 'stay out late and do not often return to their farms until 12 and one in the morning … they are much talked about'. She then claims, 'The Girls themselves, with few exceptions, do the least possible work they can.' She also complains of girls 'running away' from training centres. She suggests set timetables should be introduced at training farms, including 'Bedtime – summer 9.30pm, Bedtime – winter 9.00pm' and includes a cutting relating to Grace Smith who after being absent without leave from the Women's Army Forage Department was sentenced to fourteen days'

Top left:
Advertisement for
private purchase
working clothing
for women, 1917.

Top right:
Studio portrait of
a land girl, c. 1917.
She is proudly
showing off her
smart boots and
buskins as well
as a hint of her
breeches – this
would certainly
have been
considered risqué
before the war.

Women's Land Army armband.

Women's Land Army, Land Army Agricultural Section Proficiency badge. (Ron Franklyn)

Women's Land Army, Land Army Agricultural Section Good Service badge. (Ron Franklyn)

prison with hard labour. In her reply Miss Talbot was quick to point out the Forage Section Regulations 'do not, in my opinion, lead to desirable results' and explained such draconian measures do far more damage than good. With this sort of comment in mind, however, combined with the desire to ensure the girls were happy with their situations and were 'getting on', visiting welfare officers were appointed. Mrs Cook, the Welfare Officer for Norfolk, soon reported, 'My visits are nearly all surprise ones and never once have I found a girl in any way slacking. On the contrary they have always been hard at work, often cheerily singing over it.'

The uniform issued to the girls consisted of a knee-length overall tunic with a button-fastening integral belt, boots (orders were stringent – two pairs of working boots were all a girl would be issued a year) and gaiters or puttees, soft hat and breeches which were cut to measure for each girl. In some area clogs and leggings were supplied from the summer of 1917 and mackintoshes and jerseys from the autumn.

After three months' proficient service (of not less than 240 hours) each girl would receive her official armlet – a loden green band with a bright red crown upon it. A circular cloth badge was also awarded for passing proficiency tests in tasks such as milking, horse work, tractor driving, stacking corn, hoeing and manure spreading. Red cloth chevrons were also awarded, each chevron representing six months' work of not less than 1,440 hours – there was also a red diamond with an outline green diamond in the centre that represented two years' work. The girls started on a minimum wage of 18s a week, steadily increased to 20s and finally 22s 6d in 1919.

Despite initial scepticism, the efficient organisation and training of the Land Army girls proved their worth to the farmers. The key to the situation was that the weather also improved, food production was up and the wheat harvest of 1917 was the best in British history. Although this was a great achievement there was still a fear among many people that the country was running out of food. A Ministry of Food had been established in December 1916 but throughout 1917 the British government had been concerned about the nation's food stocks and the particular shortages in sugar, flour and potatoes but had been reluctant to impose rationing. It was suggested instead that people might wish to adopt 'The National Scale of Voluntary Rations' of 4 pounds of bread or 3 pounds of flour, 2½ pounds of meat and ¾ pounds of sugar per week. This became a matter of patriotic pride and many families signed pledges and placed pledge cards headed 'In Honour Bound' in their windows to show their support. To help the situation the County War Agricultural Committees organised food economy lectures, many of them led by members of the Women's Institute, particularly extolling the virtues of pickling vegetables and bottling fruit. Special economy recipes appeared in the newspapers, magazines and books such as *Our War-Time Kitchen Garden* by Tom Jerrold (1917), informing us not only about what we can grow in our garden but also about our dietary needs and emphasising that we can still remain 'the bull-dog breed without the roast beef of old England.'

Marginia Money

Every woman who helps in agriculture during the war is as truly serving her country as the man who is fighting in the trenches or on the sea.

President of the Board of Trade.

President of the Board of Agriculture.

Certificate of appreciation awarded to Marginia Money for services rendered in the Land Army during the First World War.

The Women's Land Army was disbanded in 1919. Meriel Talbot (made a Dame in 1920 for her services to the Board of Agriculture), Director of the Women's Land Army during the war, wrote: 'The returns (taken in 1918 of 12,637 Land Army members) showed that the work was distributed as follows: 5,734 milkers, 293 tractor drivers, 3,791 field workers, 635 carters, 260 ploughmen, 84 thatchers, 21 shepherds.' Lord Ernle, Minister of Agriculture wrote:

> The branches which have been enumerated (by the Land Army) have covered a wide field. In all of them women have excelled... In driving motor tractors they have done at least as well as men. Here also light hands tell. As drivers they have shown themselves not only skilful and enduring, but economical.

British Women! — the Royal Air Force needs your help

as **CLERKS,**
WAITRESSES
COOKS, experienced
MOTOR CYCLISTS
& in many other capacities.
Full particulars from the nearest
EMPLOYMENT EXCHANGE
ENROL AT ONCE IN THE
W·R·A·F.
WOMEN'S ROYAL AIR
FORCE

IN UNIFORM

THE MAIN forerunner of all the women's military units of the First World War was the Women's Emergency Corps (WEC), founded within two days of the declaration of war. Although it was created and led by aristocratic and upper-class ladies like the other extant or newly raised women's units of the time, the WEC soon showed itself different as it welcomed women workers from all classes into its membership. After small beginnings in the offices of the Actresses' Franchise League, after just one week it became too big for the rooms, migrated to a theatre and finally occupied commodious offices on Baker Street, London.

Early publicity was keen to point out that some of the WEC's most ardent workers were 'non-Suffragist' and it worked in association with other bodies, such as the Soldiers' and Sailors' Families' Association, the National Union of Women Workers, the Charity Organisation Society, the Young Women's Christian Association War Clubs, the Children's Care Committees, and the Women's League of Service and Schools for Mothers.

The Kitchen Department, aided by supplies from the National Food Fund, distributed in four months 28,378 meals, and 1,065 pounds of plum puddings were made before Christmas 1914. In co-operation with the National Guild of Housecraft, unemployed girls were given training in domestic work and 'handy women' were sent as helpers to various benevolent agencies.

The interpreting department of the WEC was the first organised body to assist those from Belgium. Hundreds of interpreters were enrolled; they met the continental trains at the stations and ships at the docks, provided carefully compiled lists of hotels, boarding houses and lodgings of all kinds, and investigated and arranged accommodation. The WEC were also the first to start teaching elementary French and German to the soldiers in training, and held classes in nearly fifty military centres.

The hospitality department worked tirelessly for Belgian and French refugees by supplying both lodging and clothes to those who were homeless and destitute. Some hundreds of women motorcyclists and motorists who ran their own cars and were capable of doing running repairs registered for

Opposite:
WRAF
recruitment
poster of 1918.

51

Above: Queen
Mary's Army
Auxiliary Corps
recruitment
poster, 1918.
(PST 7813)

Above right:
Studio portrait of
a member of the
Women's Legion.

the WEC Motor Department and rendered invaluable service in the early
days of the war as despatch riders and drivers.

By the end of 1914 there were branches of the Women's Emergency
Corps all over Great Britain, each one of them managed independently by its
own committee and raising its own funds. Respected for its well-organised
and high standard of work, the immediate descendant of the WEC was the
Women's Legion (WL). It was originally proposed in 1915 by the
Marchioness of Londonderry as a voluntary service to meet the shortage of
cooks and clerks in the British Army in Britain. Over 40,000 women enrolled,
and a number of sections of work were set up. Despite being uniformed, the
Women's Legion was not militaristic and did not practise drill.

When the Women's Army Auxiliary Corps (WAAC) was formed in 1917
the cooking and general service sections of WL enrolled into it while the
Women's Legion Motor Transport Service, which had been officially used
by the British Army from February 1917, recruited and organised Women's
Royal Air Force (WRAF) drivers from 1918 and carried on until 1919.

The year 1917 heralded the creation of two more uniformed military
services for women. Many local girls saw their chance to get out of the
country, seek adventure and do their bit in uniform by volunteering for

The standard hat badge of the Women's Legion.

Left: The private purchase uniform jacket and gauntlets of a Women's Legion driver, c. 1916.

service in the new women's forces of the Women's Army Auxiliary Corps or Women's Royal Naval Service (WRNS).

Raised under the control of the War Office the WAAC rapidly enrolled thousands of recruits. The first WAACs proceeded to France on 31 March 1917 (very soon the French nicknamed them 'Les Tommettes'); by early

Women's Legion recruited drivers serving with the Army Service Corps, 1918. The car is a 16-20 hp Vauxhall.

The Woman's Motor Manual of 1918.

Clerks in the Women's Army Auxiliary Corps line up to meet the queen at Wimereux, France on 6 June 1917. (IWM Q 2494)

1918, some 6,000 WAACs were there. The organisation was officially renamed Queen Mary's Army Auxiliary Corps in April 1918, and new cap badges were designed and issued, the main difference being that they were headed by a scroll with the inscription, 'Queen Mary's'. The new title was not generally adopted, however, and the WAACs proudly stayed WAACs. Be they WAACs or QMAACs their roles did not change. They served at home and abroad often working on unglamorous tasks such as lines of communication, as cooks, storekeepers, clerical workers, telephonists, drivers, and in motor vehicle maintenance.

The QMAAC was disbanded in 1921; some 57,000 women had enrolled into its ranks and though never given full military status those serving abroad had often worked close to the front line. Three of them were awarded Military Medals for bravery.

The first Wrens to appear in uniform were enrolled at the Royal Navy Depot, Crystal Palace in 1918. Most 'Wrens' were given a trade category denoted by blue non-substantive trade badges worn on the right arm; the symbols and what category they represented are as follows:

Women's Army Auxiliary Corps worker wearing the standard overall type uniform made in khaki gabardine, c. 1917. Coloured insets in their shoulder strap indicated the WAAC's section (for example, household section – red; clerical section – brown; motor drivers – claret).

Scallop shell: household workers
Three-spoked wheel: motor drivers
Arrow crossed by a lightning flash: signals
Crossed keys: storekeepers, porters and messengers
Crossed quill pens: clerical staff and accounts
Envelope: postwomen and telegraphists
Crossed hammers: technical workers
Star: miscellaneous

All of these first Wrens were deployed to shore bases or Royal Naval Air Service stations. By the end of the war Wrens could count 5,500 members, 500 of them officers. The WRNS was disbanded in 1919.

The last of the forces to recruit women into its fold was the most junior of all the forces; the newly titled Royal Air Force saw the formation of the Women's Royal Air Force in April 1918. The original intent of the WRAF was to substitute women for men in non-combatant roles and was successful

Right:
A WAAC badge.

Far right:
A QMAAC badge.

Fitness training for
WRNS at Crystal
Palace, 1918.
(IWM Q 18694)

in recruiting a sizeable number of women volunteers in a very short time to become drivers and mechanics and filling other wartime needs. Disbanded in 1920, the last veteran from this era was Gladys Powers, who died in 2008.

WRNS ratings working as mine net workers wiring glass floats, Lowestoft, 1918. (IWM Q 19640)

WRAF on parade in 1918. (IWM Q 27254)

AFTER THE WAR PROBLEMS.

Shall I still wear 'em — or shall I get married?

DEMOB AND LEGACIES

THE WOMEN'S military uniformed organisations of QMAAC, WRNS and WRAF were all disbanded by 1921; they had existed for but a few years and months but they had proved themselves proficient and very capable of the duties allotted to them – to the degree that when the winds of war blew in 1939 they were raised again with confidence, vigour and the full authority of the War Office. Conscription for women was introduced in 1941.

Although many had come under fire, some even being killed and wounded, no British woman had officially served in combat with the British Army. If you discover a photo of one of your female ancestors in male uniform, proceed with caution: there was quite a vogue for ladies to be 'daring' and have their photographs taken in their husbands' or male relatives' uniforms – a trend almost certainly started by the popular music hall male impersonator Miss Vesta Tilley. Tilley's popularity reached its all-time high point during the First World War when she and her husband ran a military recruitment drive. In the guise of characters like 'Tommy in the Trench' and 'Jack Tar Home from Sea', Tilley performed songs such as 'The army of today's all right' and 'Jolly Good Luck to the Girl who Loves a Soldier'.

The Women's Land Army also disbanded in 1919. After the war many former Land Army members had acquired the sense of adventure and took advantage of the free passage to the Dominions offered to ex-servicemen and women. It is not surprising with the positive attitude of practical contribution to country and home that many members of the Women's Land Army and food economy workers went on to become the backbone of the Women's Institutes across Great Britain. The value of the Land Army in the Great War was proved beyond doubt and, like their sisters in the military units, they proved themselves again in the Second World War.

With the return of peace the British Red Cross Society and St John Ambulance divided into two voluntary aid societies but maintained the VAD scheme through the 1920s and 1930s. Their old Ford 'Model T' ambulances, some still bearing the scars and mud of front-line service, were given a new livery in black and white with the amalgamated decals of the St John

Opposite:
The quandary
of the Land Girl:
although depicted
as a cartoon, the
sentiment was
very real at the
end of the war.

Right: Vesta Tilley in her khaki uniform.

Far right: Sarah Gamzu Gurney MBE, Commandant of the Ingham War Hospital, Norfolk. It was opened in 1914 and closed in 1918, during which time over a thousand wounded servicemen passed through the hospital.

Certificate of thanks presented to Miss Ida Lawrence, VAD.

President of the British Red Cross Society.

Grand Prior of the Order of St. John of Jerusalem in England.

PRESENTED
by the Joint Committee of the British Red Cross Society and the Order of St. John of Jerusalem in England to

Miss Ida Lawrence

in recognition of valuable services rendered during the War.

Countersigned *J. C. Davis*
Secretary

1914 - 1919.
83, Pall Mall, London.

Chairman

Evelyn Cecil.
Vice Chairman

Ambulance and Red Cross (in peacetime the Order of St John becomes the senior organisation) and became the first ambulances of the Home Ambulance Service run by the Joint Ambulance Committee. Hailed an instant and resounding success between May 1919 (when the first station was established) and the end of March 1925, over 294,415 cases had been moved by these ambulances from the 341 stations across the country. The equipment and some of the funds from the Auxiliary War Hospitals was not wasted either: it was pooled in the first depots for Red Cross medical loans so that medical items such as commodes, crutches and wheelchairs could be obtained by anyone in need, be they servicemen or civilians. Although both voluntary aid societies accepted women and both had female units there were still no mixed divisions; in many areas the trend was that the Red Cross was the female nursing branch and men joined the St John Ambulance.

Private purchase 'She did her bit on Munitions' badge, 1918.

However, the effect of the First World War on the role and status of women was far more profound. Some of the simplest things taken for granted by women today were not options for women in British society before 1914. Consider that before the First World War it was almost unknown for women to wear trousers. During the war the practicalities of wearing trousers by Munitionettes and women in factories or breeches by land girls saw the door open for all women to wear these garments but it was still considered rather daring. The same reasons of practicality and a new-found need for freedom of movement had seen the demise of the corset and the increased popularity of the 'newfangled' brassiere. Their skirts were shorter and many had cut their hair short – the glories of the 'bob' in a variety of forms carried on and was popularised in fashionable vogues throughout the 1920s and 1930s. Women became far more independent and – although some eyebrows were still raised – women could now smoke cigarettes and wear cosmetics openly, and they could visit public houses and cinemas unaccompanied by men. Women even participated in organised sports – in public. In August 1917 the first football tournament was launched for the female munition workers' teams of north-east England. Officially known as the Tyne Wear & Tees Alfred Wood Munition Girls Cup it was popularly known as 'The Munitionettes' Cup'. Certainly not swept along with the winds of change for women, the Football Association banned women's teams in December

Star, War Medal and Victory Medal (1914–15) awarded to Ella Mills VAD for service in the First World War. Trios and pairs of standard First World War service medals were awarded to all nurses and VADs who served abroad during the conflict.

Above:
AEC Munitions Factory (Beckton, London) football team, 1917–18 season.
(IWM HU 70114)

1921; undaunted, the English Ladies' Football Association was formed. Most significant of all was the Representation of the People Act, passed in 1918. This granted the vote to women over the age of thirty who were classed as householders. In 1928 this was extended to all women over twenty-one.

For the most part women had found their freedom and after the war they chose to have families and to treasure the man who had returned from the fighting and free up a place for him to return to work. Even though many of these men ended up unemployed during the Depression of the 1920s and 1930s, and although much of the promised 'Land Fit for Heroes' did not emerge, the emancipation of women had begun.

Left: One of the early Haig Fund poppies, many of which were sold by female street collectors who had lost 'their boy' in the Great War.

FURTHER READING

Adie, Kate. *Corsets to Camouflage*. Hodder & Stoughton, 2003.

Binyon, Laurence. *For Dauntless France*. Hodder & Stoughton, 1918.

Bowser, Thekla. *The Story of British VAD Work in the Great War*. 1925; Imperial War Museum reprint 2003.

Canning, John. *1914*. Odhams, 1967.

Clark-Kennedy, A. E. *Edith Cavell: Pioneer and Patriot*. Faber & Faber, 1965.

Cole Mackintosh, Lt Col Ronnie. *A Century of Service to Mankind*. Century Benham, 1986.

Collett Wadge, D. *Women in Uniform*. 1946, Imperial War Museum reprint 2003.

Davies, Norman. *Europe: A History*. Oxford University Press, 1996.

DeGroot, Gerald J. *Blighty: British Society in the Era of the Great War*. Harlow, 1996.

Fountain, Nigel (ed.). *Women at War*. Michael O'Mara, 2002.

Fraser, Helen. *Women and War Work*. Arnold Shaw, 1918.

Lawrence, Dorothy. *Sapper Dorothy Lawrence: The Only English Woman Soldier, Late Royal Engineers, Fifty-First Division 179th Tunneling Company*. J. Lane, 1919.

Lee, Janet. *War Girls: The First Air Nursing Yeomanry in the Great War*. Manchester University Press, 2005.

MacDonald, Lyn. *The Roses of No Man's Land*. Michael Joseph, 1980.

Marlow, Joyce (ed.). *The Virago book of Women and the Great War*. Virago, 1998.

Marwick, Arthur. *Women at War 1914–1918*. Fontana, 1977.

Priestly, J. B. *The Edwardians*. Heinemann, 1970.

Reader, W. J. *At Duty's Call: A Study in Obsolete Patriotism*. Manchester University Press, 1988.

Riley-Smith, Jonathan. *Hospitallers: The History of The Order of St John*. Hambledon Press, 1999.

Ryder, Rowland. *Edith Cavell*. Hamish Hamilton, 1975.

Sandes, Flora. *An English Woman-Sergeant in the Serbian Army*. Hodder & Stoughton, 1916.

Sandes, Flora. *The Autobiography of a Woman Soldier: A Brief Record of Adventure with the Serbian Army 1916–1919*. H. R. & G. Witherby, 1927.

Terry, Roy. *Women in Khaki*. Columbus, 1988.

Trollope, Joanna. *Britannia's Daughters*. Hutchinson, 1983.

Ward, Irene. *FANY Invicta*. Hutchinson, 1955.

Wheelwright, Julie. *Amazons and Military Maids*. Pandora, 1999.

Wilson, Trevor. *Myriad Faces of War: Britain and the Great War 1914–18*. Polity Press, 1986.

Wood, Emily. *The Red Cross*. Dorling Kindersley, 1995.

INDEX

Figures in italics refer to illustrations

Actresses' Franchise League 51
Air raids, 13, 17–18, 20
Ambulance 9, 11, 12, 19, 25, 34, 59, 61
Anderson, Louisa Garrett 7
Arm band 6, 19, 24, 25; Women's Land Army 48
Army Nursing Service 15
Army Service Corps 43, 45, 53
Attleborough, Norfolk 28
Awards and decorations 9, 11, 12, 13, 49, 60, 61
Auxiliary War Hospitals 19–28, 21, 27, 28, 61
Badge 'On War Service' 40, 41
Baines, Sister 18
Balkans War 7
Banbury National Filling Factory (NFF) 40
Belgian Army 8, 9, 11
Belgian Refugees 5–6, 6, 51
Board of Agriculture and Fisheries 43, 45
Board of Trade 31, 43
Brassard, protection 24–5
British Legion 62
Cambridge Scientific Instrument Co. 41
'Canaries' 40–1
Cavell, Edith 29, 29
Certificates of service (Land Army) 49; Red Cross & St John 60
Charity Organisation Society 51
Chisholm, Mairi 9–11
Class 7, 20, 33, 38, 46, 51
Coal heavers 37
Conductresses, omnibus 34
Cordite, exposure to 41
County War Agricultural Committees 43, 49
Dawson Scott, Mrs 7
'Devil's porridge' 37
Dornock Munition Factory 41
Downham Market, Norfolk 27
Dundee, Scotland 33
English Ladies' Football Association 61
Ernle, Lord, Minister of Agriculture 49
Etaples Hospital 17, 18, 19, 20
'Feeding the guns' 35
Fielding, Lady Dorothy 11
Field workers 41, 49
First Aid Nursing Yeomanry (FANY) 7, 8–10, 8, 9, 10, 13
Food Production Department (FPD) 43–4
Football 61, 62
Football Association 61

Forage Corps 42
Fountains Fever Hospital, Lower Tooting 29
French, Field Marshal Sir John 32
French Refugees 51
Gahan, Chaplain Sterling 29
Gleason, Mrs Helen 11
Grantham Constabulary 31
Great Eastern Railway 36
Gretna, His Majesty's Factory 37, 40
Gretna Munitionette 40
Grouitch, Mabel 11
Gurney, Sarah Gamzu 60
Haldane Reforms 15
Haverfield, the Hon. Evelina 7
Henham Hall, Suffolk 27
Home Ambulance Service 61
Home Front civilian occupations for women 31–5
Home Office, Factory Department 32
Hospital 'blues' 25–6
Identity cards 6, 24, 25, 39
Indian Nursing Service 15
Inglis, Elsie 7, 8, 13
Interpreters 51
Jackson, Lady Mather 47
Jackson, Postwoman Violet 35
Jerrold, Tom 49
Jute mills 33
King Albert of Belgium 11
Knocker, Elsie (Baroness T'Serclaes) 10–11, 10
Kragujevac, Serbia 11
Lamarck Hospital 8–9
Lancashire & Yorkshire Railway 34
'Land Fit for Heroes' 62
Landswoman, The 45
Lawrence, Ida 60
London County Council Ambulance Corps 34
Londonderry, Marchioness of 7, 52
Licensed Vehicle Workers, London & Provincial Union of 33
Lloyd George, David 32
Metropolitan Asylums Board 33–4
Mills, Ella 61
Ministry of Food 48
Ministry of Munitions 32, 35, 40
Money, Marginia 49
Monmouthshire War Agricultural Committee 47
Moore, Decima 7
Motorcyclists 11, 51
'Munitionettes' 3, 30, 32, 35–41, 38, 39, 40
Munro, Dr Hector 9
Murray, Dr Flora 7
National Explosives Factories (NEF) 36
National Filling Factory (NFF), Banbury 40
National Food Fund 51

National Guild of Housecraft 51
National Scale of Voluntary Rations 49
National Service Scheme 34
'National Shell Overall' 39
National Union of Women Workers 51
Neuve Chapelle, France 32
Newmarket racecourse 6
Norwich Cathedral 29
Paget, Almeric, Military Massage Corps 7
Paris, France 8, 13
Passchendaele 16
Patriotic duty 5–7, 31, 49
Pembrey, Carmarthenshire 36
Pembroke and Montgomery, Countess of 7
Pervyse, Women of 9–11, 10
Ploughmen 49
Plum puddings 51
Plumer, General 13
Poppy Day 62
Postwoman 31
Powers, Gladys 56
Proficiency badges, Land Army 48
Proficiency tests, Land Army 48
Queen Alexandra's Imperial Military Nursing Service (QAIMNS) 15, 16
Queen Alexandra's Royal Navy Nursing Service 15, 16
Queen Mary's Auxiliary Army Corps 52, 55, 56, 59
Railway, occupations for women 34, 34, 36
Recruitment 4, 5, 6, 6, 7, 15, 19, 45, 51, 52, 59
Red Cross 5, 9, 11, 15–29, 24, 25, 59–61
Red Cross Hospitals – see Auxiliary War Hospitals
Representation of the People Act 61–2
Royal Automobile Club Owner Drivers' War Service Corps 33
Sandes, Flora 11–12, 12
Serbian campaign 11–13
Serbian English Field Hospital 12
Serbian Relief Fund 11
'Shells Scandal' 32
Silvertown Munitions Factory explosion 40
Silver War Badge 6
Shipyard, occupations for women 33
St John Ambulance 11, 15–16, 18–20, 20, 22, 25, 59–61
Scottish Women's Hospitals 7
Soldiers' and Sailors' Families Association 51
Smith, Edith 31
Smith, Grace 47
Stobart, Mrs Mabel St Clair 7, 11, 12, 13
Talbot, Miss Meriel 45, 47, 48, 49

Territorial Force 5, 15, 16, 17
Territorial Force Medical Service 15
Territorial Force Nursing Service 15, 16, 17, 17
Thatchers 49
Tilley, Vesta 59, 60
Timber Supply Department 43
Titchfeld, Marchioness of 7
Tommettes, Les 53
Tractor drivers 49
Trade badges (non substantive for WRNS) 55
Tramway Workers 33, 36
Trousers and breeches 32, 33, 34, 37, 38, 40, 41, 46–7, 58, 61
Voluntary Aid Detachments (VAD) 14, 15–29, 17, 19, 24, 27, 59, 60–1
Voting rights 62
Wages 21, 34, 38, 41, 45, 48
War Office 7, 15, 53, 59
Welfare Officer 48
White feathers 6
Women's Agriculture Committees 45
Women's Army Auxiliary Corps 52, 53–5, 54, 55, 56
Women's Defence Relief Corps 7
Women's Emergency Corps 7, 51–2
Women's Farm and Garden Union 43
Women's Forage Corps 43
Women's Forestry Corps 43
Women's Hospital Corps 7, 13
Women's Institutes 49, 59
Women's Land Army 43–9, 58, 59
Women's League of Service 51
Women's Legion 52–3, 52, 53
Women's Legion Motor Transport Service 52
'Women's March Through London' 32
Women's National Land Service Corps (Women's Land Corps) 43
Women's Police Volunteers (WPV) 31
Women's Royal Air Force (WRAF) 50, 51, 52, 55, 57, 59
Women's Royal Naval Service 53, 55, 56, 57, 59
Women's Sick and Wounded Convoy Corps 7, 11
Women's Suffrage Societies, National Union of 6, 31
Women's Volunteer Reserve 7
Woolwich Arsenal 38, 39
Young Men's Christian Association YMCA 5
Young Women's Christian Association War Clubs 51